A Name That Is Mine

Mbuh Tennu Mbuh

Langaa Research & Publishing CIG
Mankon, Bamenda

Publisher
Langaa RPCIG
Langaa Research & Publishing Common Initiative Group
P.O. Box 902 Mankon
Bamenda
North West Region
Cameroon
Langaagrp@gmail.com
www.langaa-rpcig.net

Distributed in and outside N. America by African Books Collective
orders@africanbookscollective.com
www.africanbookscollective.com

ISBN-10: 9956-550-10-8

ISBN-13: 978-9956-550-10-4

© Mbuh Tennu Mbuh 2019

Table of Contents

Preface

A colleague once criticised my decision to do prefaces for my works, arguing that I seem to be either doing or facilitating the critic's work. While the point may be valid if we consider cases where the writer corrupts the textual composition by engaging in simplistic translations of various kinds, including proverbs, idiomatic expressions, lexical items, and so on, the prefatory statement in fact opens up the field of analysis, provides insights into the authorial closet by exploiting the meta contexts that feed the work, thereby enriching the debate. In my defence, naturally, I further tried to justify the fact that the explicatory merit of the endeavour may be more realistic in its reliance on lived experiences that may surpass the often artistic technicalities of the text itself. In this third volume of my poetry, I find that need even more urgently an imperative against the gloss of patriotic fervour that clouds our social data of becoming.

I am hoping that the reader took note of the collective pronoun, 'our', if only because from the formal beginnings of human history, the phenomenon of naming has played a cardinal role in the negotiation of identities. Yet, claims over the name have gained more legitimacy today than perhaps at any time in recorded history, partly due to the hyper-visibility in almost all sectors of human interaction. Right from antiquity, naming has always implied the right to self-identify, or, alternatively, the subtle means of a hegemonic order by which the control of individual and public spheres was/is ensured. Empires were consequently erected on the basis of this notion, appropriating cultural archetypes, renaming whole cultures in some cases, just as the eventual collapse of such structures was not unconnected to resistance from the constrained space or psyche.

The scramble for Africa by European monarchies toward the end of the 19th century was to prove perhaps the most deterministic example of naming on the global frontier. Traditional markers in every context were violated and trashed in the interest of burgeoning Empire. Eventual devolution of power to indigenous leadership was a mere symbolic gesture that concretised the perpetuation of what had been achieved by the colonising powers because the new leaders who emerged at 'independence' were anything but independent: they were poor clones of the colonial mind-set, with instructions to certify the imperialistic fraternity through the signing of crippling colonial agreements that virtually auctioned the nation-state to controllers of futures. The economic pun here is deliberate and suggests a kinship between temporality and dividends.

As a panellist at the 2018 edition of the Yaounde International Book Fair, I was seduced by the views of a co-panellist who elaborated on the fact that Cameroon was one of only few countries in the world where identification of its 'parts' was based on the cardinal points of the compass and only mutated accordingly. To privilege abstract geography in this way, to the detriment of its human variant which encompasses socio-cultural nuances, is to legitimise cultural nullity at the same time that questionable frames of reference are hailed in an authoritative show of patriotism.

Anglophone resistance in Cameroon is the result of this institutionalised collusion. It challenges and possibly marks the end of post-Empire configurations of territory in Africa. We had already seen formative agitations in Biafra, Katanga, and most recently in what emerged as South Sudan. The first two examples marked instabilities in the postcolony, to which we may add Eritrea, and Western Sahara, plagued as they were by neo-colonial hangovers that typified the mimic status of independence. Yet they also shed significant light on the limits of tele-guided diplomacy—or the failure of decolonisation, as Gayatri Spivak would phrase it technically—wherein ideological hegemony replicates itself in the guise of a bilateral entente.

We now know better, and nothing best describes this awareness than the demise of the Bollore 'Empire' in (Francophone) Africa, which had substituted formal imperial strategy, representatively, from the old centre. France, like the United Kingdom, the United States, and Germany, had disguised their presence in the formal colony by propping up individuals—call them sole proprietors from elementary pedagogy—and their evolving multi-nationals with every bit of diplomatic energy, which accounts for why the Bollore franchise suddenly had such enormous influence over the economies of especially Francophone Africa. But in Bollore's imminent downfall, the blame-game machinery in Africa's most conspicuous media outfit was activated as if we had been asleep while the Paris-backed weevil sneaked into the barn; and as if we are ignorant of Achebe's perceptive comment that a stranger does not discover our homestead without the assistance of a kinsman. Indeed, Monsieur Bollore was simply the trouble that invades your home and you beg of it to leave because there is no seat, and it reminds you: don't worry, I came with my seat.

Same with names and naming: when they are affixed in palliatives of patriotism—with their concurrent nightmare of *la Patrie*—legitimate difference is overwritten in a crass endorsement of a nationalist fraternity. The authoritative nuisance thus authenticates itself by disregarding epithetic values of relative culturalism, instead refining this into a symbolic slippage that empowers a new centre within what is obviously an internally colonial concoction.

Now, in the case of Southern Cameroons, there is an interesting difference from the usual binaries that characterise postcolonial analyses of the Self and Other. For instance, the analysis of this paradigm in any assessment of how Anglophone consciousness has evolved in Cameroon is no longer the simple equation testimony of facts and figures. Interpretive mirages, cultural nuances, the clash of ideological manhoods, and Machiavellian aesthetics have been asserted into a definition of Anglophoneness and its historicity, to the extent that a mimic-camouflage had been authenticated by the establishment as genuine. No wonder then that we started hearing of 'bilingual Anglophones' in Cameroon, a terrible conflation of data which was/is meant to serve a puerile ego of the Nation-State. This translates at best into a Franglophone mentality which was strategically being showcased as a logical substitute to the nagging dual consciousness that seems to have finally falsified the very thing it affirms, care of the elitist garb in which bilingualism is propagated in Cameroon.

This was the case until Common Law lawyers and Anglophone teachers' trade unions lifted the whitewashed lid on what had been forged as Yaounde's Pandora box. Even then, clumsy chauvinism was still blinded by its celebration of ideological stasis as patriotic norm. And now we know—that is, if we appeared not to know before—that a definition of the Anglophone in Cameroon defies dictionary and ideological simplicities. For, old Anglo-French rivalries, together with their Caucasian ancestries, are in play here; the very nature of colonial identities are new subject matter for interrogation; indigenous realism asserts itself against the formal and mega-status of boundary-makers; cultural relativism finally encodes its essence against the authoritative legacy in whitewash and gloss; even as doubts remain (they always do) as to whether a new configuration can overcome huddles to its visibility which are imposed not necessarily by constituted landlords of global power, but also by clashing egos of a neo-mimic mentality.

This threat is defined mainly through intolerance and vulnerability to the vagaries of those who still control the flow of arms. It has been so since the white man left and we discovered, but failed to acknowledge the fact, that indeed, as Ayi Kwei Armah reminds us in graphic representations of a crudely cloned mentality, the beautyful ones *were* not yet born. The grammar has changed, and took us by surprise because indolence had also taken us hostage, and its stagnating frills were often celebrated as the manifestation of a gold medal state of fulfilment.

The greatest legacy of our struggle is the idea of Anglophoneness from the contingencies of history: our existentialist status is a truth that can never be negotiated, never denied. A tempting parallel to this line of argument is the fate of the Jews and their resilience under Roman authority, as dramatized in the William Wyler film *Ben Hur*. When the new Tribune, Messala, is sent to Judea with instructions to transform it 'into a more obedient and disciplined province', his enthusiasm is however checked when Sextus (a long-serving administrator in the provine) reminds him that 'You can break a man's skull, you can arrest him, you can throw him into a dungeon', and then poses a fundamental question: 'But how do you control what's up here [taps his head]? How do you fight an idea, especially a new idea?' The 'idea' of Anglophone in Cameroon is not new; but it has been perennially renewed.

An indicator to the religious fervour that characterises affinity to Anglophoneness in Cameroon is the declaration of the one-time Minister of Communication, Professor

Kontchou Komeni, that the Social Democratic Party, SDF, was a religion in the North West Region. A metonymic understanding of notional Anglophone in Cameroon, whether of Bamenda or Buea, further suggests ideological signification in mental assertiveness in this regard, and we have been asking the same question repeatedly—'How do you fight an idea'— since 1972, at least. To betray this idea, that is kill the hope that a people have of themselves, without any precondition, is to condemn them to eternal slavery. History books remind us of such traitors whose fifteen minutes of fame may span decades of hollow manhood, yet they always end up like the miserable scum of humanity, sneaking into the sewage of their neglect, detested by even scavengers, while their progeny is doomed to pass the mark of Cain down the line. Every Southern Cameroon leader and freedom fighter must reflect on this.

It can also be argued that even the most politically correct observer must have felt genuinely uncomfortable at one point with the way things were going on in the national triangle. But that is only how far it went. And today, enabling arguments have been accumulated from forward-looking constituents, only that the arrogance of those who control the microphone of State makes them to think they can circumvent the dissemination of truth no more as an authoritative discourse but as the Achebean dancing mask with perspectival implications on interpretation and meaning. Bad faith, which resulted from the pupil modifying the exam question through Commissions that were never factored into the equation, becomes key to the rationalisation of wrong. Similarly, resource persons who were seen to have been talking too inconveniently, were displaced into such Commissions.

****

In a struggle like The Coffin Revolution in Cameroon, cultural awareness is imperative and its development must recognise a spiritual base. The problem with African development is partly the fact that our spiritual conduits were strangled during the formal colonial era while we simultaneously hailed, and continue to hail, alien versions. The rationalism of Ezeulu in Chinua Achebe's *Arrow of God* was overtaken by the neglect and mimic vision of post-independence leadership, eventually catapulting us into a beggarly condition that can easily be taken as natural and terminal. Ezeulu's decision for his son, Oduche, to serve as his eyes and ears in the white man's establishment was a perceptive position in the multicultural future to which Africa was being exposed in a radical way.

Naturally, the bullying ideology of the coloniser saw this objectivity as a threat to his own immanence, and ensured that the son, a prince in his traditional right, was brainwashed into the typical enemy in the house. The lineage of Ezeulu is finally compromised the same way that David's was by the Romans, whose humiliating banner, 'King of the Jews', undermined the functional historicity which Jesus embodied, contextually.

Now, in the shifting landscape of the Anglophone imagination in Cameroon, notably since 2016, a radical demographic emerged unannounced, defied constituted expectations, and bannered its own coffin as a counter to the Christ-Oduche manipulation by authoritarian cheer-gatherers. The Struggle, ever since, has been staged on a cultural turf, with implications that gather around a name. Interestingly, the debate—especially as propagated by pseudo-historians on the conservative fringe—has attempted to deny the colonial mapping of the Cameroons, some even arguing along a so-called Republican trajectory of a '*ni Anglophone, ni Francophone*'. This is simply ridiculous because you cannot downplay a linguistic identity by using its constitutional rival in your favour! And what is more, doing so only when it is convenient for you.

A name is intrinsically linked to culture, and as postcolonial subjects, we cannot advocate a purist identity, in search of a way forward: smears of the past also mark us, and in claiming our cultural heritage, we have to acknowledge such composite hybridity, inspired by Kwasi Wiredu's philosophical proposition, without being mimics of the colonial, neo-colonial, and post-independence sentence. After 1884, it was clear that our previous Nations underwent a form of conurbation whose new root was eventually located beneath the Fako. To recognise and affirm this, we must be wary of the Nwoyes and Oduches, whose progeny—whether as Obi Okonkwo in *No Longer at Ease* or (in an analogous context) Samba Diallo in *Ambiguous Adventures*—risk introducing their virused nomenclatures into our evolved and evolving historicity.

For, indeed, a people who do not deny their cultural root will always find their place in the world, however dispersed they may be. Their root always connects them to the furthest realms of existence, where truth is lodged. The Jews are blessed in the ordinary sense of the word because they have stubbornly affirmed their God through their myth of creation. The Romans tried to frustrate this effort and the most they could do was format a new version of that myth in the form of the New Testament, which has then been universalised into a colonialist trope. Ironically, the Jews have distanced themselves from the Roman gloss.

****

When some years back, in the columns of *The* POST (Nos. 0319 and 0321) I had reflected on a contemporary worry under the caption 'I, A Southern Cameroonian—So What?—And Political Symbolization in Cameroon', it did not occur to me then that a nose-dive scenario could be so crassly stage-managed on the national scene and in the name of patriotism. We now know that even the Patriot eventually gets bored with lactational pedagogy that formats the mind into a convenience of doldrums, unaware that indeed, you can never fool all the people all the time. The emphasis by the political elite on the indivisibility of the whole testifies to the convenience with which history has been doctored in this petering establishment. What more can we say today to demystify this dated cloak of neo- and internal colonialism, after Bernard Fonlon had already philosophised over its irrelevance in his iconoclastic article, 'Res Una Publica', published in *Abbia* of May 1982?

This was a special issue meant to celebrate the 10th anniversary of the Unitary State. Arguing that 'after ten years of its existence … we take it for granted that we know what a United Republic is', Fonlon then asserts that: 'A thing is said to be One by this[,] that it is not divided in itself but divided, separate from [e]very thing else: internal whole, external separation. It can therefore stand up to be counted. Internal individuality, external uniqueness—these are the intrinsic notes of oneness'. Needless to say that as 'Africa in miniature', Cameroon lacks even the shadowy credentials of such a unique 'personality'. That edition of *Abbia* was predictably banned after the political and intellectual Squealers whom Ngugi wa Thiongo depicts in *Wizard of the Crow* as caricatures of our postcolonial condition quickly simplified Fonlon's philosophical rendition of our national abortion to the Grand Camarad. Barely three years or so later, Fon Gorji Dinka was to face a similar humiliation after he pointed out that the nomenclature of the State had been tampered with. And today, finally, we know the faces that are behind the mask, which Tebid Mongwa tried to theorise in a neo-patriotic tribute to the State.

A Name that is Mine is therefore a confession and a hope: how we, either as individuals or as a people, participated in forging the embarrassing historicity on the one hand, and on the other, that things can still be better. Victor Epie Ngome's *Weka* is the archetypal precursor of such hope, and her voice sutures Bangem and Ngemba scars into a new horizon of representation, possibly the final frontier of our postcolonial nightmare. But even hope, like a dream, must be laboured for, each day its testimony, into unknown futures. The endeavour is, and must remain, that of dream-builders, the only fixed material being resolute aspiration, because its frontiers are never determined by calculated data.

And this is where we risk compromising our dream-future, whether as Anglophone Cameroonians or as Southern Cameroonians. I make this observation with pain in my heart because of the observed vagrancy that has characterised the mapping out of Anglophone manhood since November 2016. There is a dangerous demographic crisis that must be addressed, else we metamorphose into the eternal laughing stock of postcolonial abortions. In sounding like this, I am however comforted by the representative plaintiff call to order by Barrister Bobga Harmony (and later, in Washington DC and Berlin), following the confusion in the leadership blocs of Southern Cameroon/Ambazonia. No one voice can represent the aspiration of the People without even the semblance of a constitutional base. Granted that we are still in the formative stages of this process, there must be a degree of mutual respect and sanity within the ranks of our interim leaders.

A disturbing trend (until the DC meeting) is that we risk making the vital people-oriented energy, which has been galvanised for this Cause, to dissipate in online muscling and puerile narcissism. Southern Cameroon independence will never come from the internet alone, if at all. Of course, we can, and should quarrel, but with a legitimate and patriotic focus. Often, it is necessary, and even healthy, to disagree in a struggle like ours. But we should not quarrel in public, where our detractors are waiting to exploit such moments against our legitimate Cause. Where is the roof that should hide our differences from the preying stranger? Such a stranger, as the saying goes in the village, only causes confusion in our ranks in order to snatch our yam. And I dare to say that if we cannot moderate our individual egos, then we will merely be fighting for an alternative nightmare. Today, it is the common man/woman on Ground Zero who is caught in the crossfire, unable to understand who to trust amongst the blocs of interest (which Ni John Fru Ndi expanded upon after his own adduction on April 28, 2019 to include militia sponsored by some government officials), all hailing him/her as their shield of legitimacy.

When the Coffin Revolution started in late 2016, it was easy to foresee the clash of egos threatening the very hope which we try to garner today. Anglophone Cameroon writing (a redundant tag, some may say) has recorded the rush of adrenalin in tears and hopes, aware of the foolhardiness of rushing into emotional moments and brandishing a partisan manifesto uncritically; just as he or she will need to beware of conservative seductions that are rallied at such moments with the aim of defusing the teeming energy. Such a threat could be seen in online postings, where virtual punches generally hurt our resolve and leave the detractor more entrenched in enacting Auzwitch superlatives in culture-cleansing.

Vindicated as such by the selfishly clashing egos amongst those who should focus, at the least, on the Cause, rather than be distracted into bloc or personalised byways, one feels terribly lost in a sense of exile where we stand. At such moments, one finally understands the misery of Ayi Kwei Armah's archetypal Teacher in *The Beautyful Ones Are Not Yet Born*, whose enthusiasm during the anti-colonial struggle in Ghana too soon withers into a neo-colonial nightmare, forcing him to become an unwilling recluse. When we meet Teacher in the novel, he is sitting in the significantly ritual pose of Mahatma Gandhi, listening to music from the Congo. These are songs of sorrow, but also of patriotism and hope, compromised by a mediocre post-independence leadership that was beautifully satirised by Franco in his song, 'Lumumba, l'Hero Nationale'.

Reflecting on the shifting paradigm of post-independence leadership, then, one cannot help but wonder about the path ahead for Anglophone Cameroon, aka Southern Cameroons/Ambazonia. Before 2016, we had managed to endure what was clearly a case of internal colonialism; braving decades of stigma, name-calling, and every archetypal innuendo of othering; tolerating Anglophone leaders who were, and are still, aping authoritarian mores and their ridiculous fanfare, unaware of the changing demographics in their various constituencies; and so on. And now that things have been going the way they have been going, with the cream of the new Anglophone leadership in jail, we cannot afford to still get the confused rationalisation of personalised agendas from those we expect to be steering the boat for the simple reason that this is a collective struggle. While there has hardly been a liberation struggle that bases its vision on consensus, it is also true that our leaders, especially those of them who are not yet incarcerated, should not be charting an alternative doom for us.

We need to make a difference from South Sudan, and stop aiming at each other's foot for supremacy. Even the next-door case of Biafra may serve as a timely reminder. In *Behind the Rising Sun*, S. O. Mezu depicts enthusiastic leaders of Biafra crisscrossing Europe and popping champagne and enriching themselves, while millions were being slaughtered on the ground. How can we be more than this, not just because we have to be, imperatively, but also because our goal is more than the mere vagaries of materialist bliss? Where is our Oscar Schindler who may be sticking his neck out just to safe one descendant of Weka, eventually?

The beauty of dreams is that they always lead us on, always on, across sloughs of despond, into enabling vistas for our future, if only we do not blunder and transform them into nightmares. With this in mind, and given the urgency of the situation, we can only do one of two things now: remain under the given name, and in this case be forever vulnerable to the manipulations of the slave master and name-giver; or stand and talk as one, affirming the name that is ours!

MTM
Bamenda,
May 1, 2019.

'Our lands were ravaged;
We seek a new beginning'
          - Apocalypto

'...how many years can some people exist
Before they're allowed to be free?'
          - Bob Dylan

The Beginning

is never known, only
a recipe for myth,
the yarn of memory and yardstick of
presence-in-approximation; and of conquest
when mal-stewed;

the comfort zone for the reinvention of meaning,
also, in the camouflage of fraternity

after which roadblocks may grow
on brow of the dispossessed, the strident
clamour back to the future,
if poorly managed, because

storytellers are despised on virtual frontiers
of a macabre vision on sand.

Song of Your Nemesis

Long after the beautyful ones were aborted at dawn
in roots manger of a different ism
and the hired Squealers intoned new hallelujahs
in the panel-beated triangle, chanting self-praise,
fraudsters conjured a tropical Xanadu, a programmed mess
for cloned Oximandias, king of kings,
hugging these shards of eminence
refracted against plebeian hope on Mungo shrine.

But I, your nemesis, all said and done, at toll-time of
            reckoning
when excess of stress hardens my hurting soul:
how else do I celebrate myself now—me,
my forebear, my progeny by the riotous banks
of the Mungo—against the propagated fraud, stepping away
from the kaleidoscopic paradise you conjured in a shaded
            conclave,
now projected in sequences of cuddled blood
and fear; the blood of a daughter raped and raped
again, and again, by guards of the nation;
fear from the death-cry of a son whose next-in-line
dreams ended with a bullet from guards of the nation:
all this and so much more?

Fear is no more, and beyond its cunning frontiers
the sun smiles in balms of hope, because
those who are pushed into the ditch
also know what it means to be rich.

I have lost faith in the glory of the fatherland,
as you see it, now that my tears drop on the withered garland

knowing that only dreams give me a name
that is mine, my story by the river bank that is same.

It is suffering unmerited that makes a heart of stone, when
excess of stress liberates the hurting soul:
we are the survivors in rusted chains re-crossing the Mungo,
toiling and heaving against burdens of pseudo-kinship.

This noon silence shatters the pods of peace in my garden,
and the cockcrow cautions the resurrection of more traitors
offering lipless smiles on cine-space, their gorgon charmers
rehearsing the drills that bring down the mighty,
after the town crier relates the message in the market place.

My wings stir and then flap, stir and
flap for a phoenix mystery and horizon;
hovering over my sorrow, energised for a name that is mine:
no more the constructed lie…
no more the pampered iniquities…
no more the asphyxiating choruses in *asimba*!—but not
          asimbonaga—
no more the name-givers who insist on a surname
with spikes of phallic hallelujah
because I claim the name that is mine, forever…

Memory (form across the River)

These wrinkled hands you once loved,
Their warmth many a stormy night dissolved;

But lingering doubts from foul whispers
Diseased our tryst after which kin vipers

(And fed by your sudden inconstancy,
When you hearkened to sirens across the sea

As smoked tadpoles spiced my *achu'* at dusk
With thoughts of your glowing face in musk)

Toasted green-eyed orgies, a requiem overture
With nothing more, after your willed fall, to capture.

More than Tongue Can Tell

Rural pedagogy back in the 70s unravels the mystery of today
after diviners collapsed at the point of knowledge,
weeping at gorgon-images astride the grave.

Atrocities unspeakable
verged on sandy banks of the nation
before the return of exiled patriots,
when the national brass band
concocts Mozart's requiems
over strewn petals, a national tear.

But how did it come then that a people-awake
pampered Ali Baba clones—their glistening torsos
betray their kind—who auctioned the ovary to their cartel?

Slain patriots foresaw the stab in the spiced phallic-talk
by regime Squealers whose tonton macoute gangs
fed carbide to new agitators on frontline;
and lobbied the surrendered soul of the nation
with *gombo* lip-oiling, a new pedagogy,
when even dons learn how to scratch hydra backs

in return for engine-saw kisses, and call it *njangi*,
the yardstick for preferment, when hoary godfathers
diagnose patriotic doom in their pantheon, speechless.

A Name that I Know

Once I was tempted by the frills of sophistication,
rootless nomenclatures, generally, divesting me of
echoes from shrine conduits which call to cottoned ears.

A Christian name, I tell you verily, is short cut
to nullity, self-effaced by ruffian thought with incense,
grafting other contrinames on my roots:
the last of the apostles (for instance) who never knew
the Messiah, like the rest of them, but sutured
to my shadow; or Psaul, the crafty man of God
with the blood of innocence dripping from his sword
in a Roman regiment, a turn-coater—
let me feel the name I know, coursing
through my blood, rooted to centuries of felt need;
salute the ancestral spark, rekindled
in new dawns even at android crossroads,
a rainbow lore and a vision;

then God will stand by me, West of the Mungo,
paddle me across ancestral waves, the breakers
nurturing my hurt heart,
before the men from the East rehearse
their earth-cleansing rituals
because the name at baptism is not mine anymore.

When the Gods stand by you, in truth,
no Auschwitz mass-servant can put out the candle
which shows the way across vales of memory
and of misery from the hate-swelled lips of
my fake *vrai semblable*—the binge acolytes, sneaking
in and out of shaded joints, hailing the tilting nation,

imagining a future from invented space
and a graft-name with no birth certificate.

Still Waiting for Doom

From echoes of the second coming
at brink of day's end, amidst
the usual chaos of how not to die
too soon or too poor,
snorting in mimed gourmandism at primetime
cheerled by the Archangels of Monekoo
and chorused by the Youth Choir of Tabeken,
a dizzying entrée;

but the cheer of welcome
was too soon fuddled in sulphur sheets
of lotus fragrance, the failing grunts
of new patriots renewing vows;

such watery-mouth halleluiah acolytes
whose Wakiri trots from phallic spires of Notre Dame
to igneous Ngoaekele was the century's nightmare, dragging
their robes of rare silk and craft in patriotic mud

because the national ovary
became a new mine for cloned patriots
parroting vows, sluggish like their trailing gowns,
watching the setting sun
with a lapsed grin, and still to learn

that change defies trimmed agendas,
fits itself when least expected
and they celebrate a snail fancy,
scaling dream-heights, in wait.

Oath of New Patriots

Clenched fists, pumping skywards, had designed
today's dream, now meshed in
plastic patriotism of spiritual eunuchs,
searching for the sun;

languorous slogans, mal-seasoned in vinegar,
from bald-heads of steel, but
whose new, blackened hair, and
fed with a shot of something I don't know up the arm,
cannot forestall tomorrow's imperatives,

and how they sniff at crumbling pillars,
the ruined phallusgate of their future,

not ours, anymore!

Mystory

Your chequered narrative in vain glee
Conjured cocoon visions in my valley of green,
A stumpy moment which I dread, and wonder
How it endured these decades of barren grey.

Now you must listen to me and my tale
Of abortive kinship, collateral impasse in Paris-
London *conjoncture*, forced to hate the world that was
Mine at dodokido moment of the naming ceremony.

Forged in amber zones, and forever cast in neon
Flares, we celebrate the feast of welcome, heaving
Ogun mysteries on Zulu toes (our emissaries), cast
In image of Fako atavus, rubbing Weka's navel, ever gently.

But you are blind even to meet and mate, when the birds
        roost,
Blinded by your bloated ego and mercenary advisor,
Tutored by stories not yours: where, your shrines of remorse
If not desecrated in vagrant ententes and crass auctions?

I look into your red orbs and see no kin, but an octopus
        stretch
Whose dread I've learned to tame to shame; your raspy voice
Hoarsely patching endless erratas of your blunder, as I launch
        my boat
On a Mungo breaker, paddling for my bank, O, for a new
        year!

A Song of Freedom

When I, too, sing Anglophone
in this njamboland, this petering island of writing
things in cine-glory, where the verse-maker must surrender
to chronic falsehood re-fashioned, or be tenant
in dungeon chambers where stone-breaking is an art
in gangsters' curriculum,

may History triumph over Ideology

as every iota of my blood
drops
to purify
the muddied river, our Babylon,
along and besides which,

from Genesis to these revelations,

we mirror ourselves not as mirrored,
but
in Weka renaissance of tearful aftermaths
and staged brotherhoods, concocted by the hired brains,

as a new chorus rises with the tides, energised
by dirges from Alepo and Sanna, and humming,
courage brethren, courage sisthren
you may stumble as soldiers on the front,
but cling not to pity's sluggish end
gesticulating with hailed cloth on bowfront
over the grey landmark of doom,
learning the first steps of freedom.

The Patriot

This land of hope and demons, my burden;
of crass monsters
screeching through the petering slopes
 as proof of addiction to foreign designs;

Ah, the patriot's plight
shouldering the histories of resistance,
abortive insurrections
and a thousand other schemed dreams:

yet, unaware that the barn is emptied by multi-
throat nyamfukahs, the season's
miraculous apparition, perennially revived
by plebeian blood and sweat
at precipitated ballots

in this blessed piece of barren souls
fidgeting in cockpit area
like kids and candy on volcano
nursing dreams of fatherland?

Blame You!

You forged the anger in me,
the fumes of insanity and brimstones
of the Apocalypse
spewed as Fako grudge;

and now the tentacles of hate
root in your eyes, flames of Damocles
on a doomed morning, wondering
what happened to the aeons of promise
wasted like one pinching from his mortgaged pocket

because my ship sets sail at high tide, to universal acclaim,
the rippling breakers soothing my heartaches.

The choice had been yours, the glee of abuse,
when you refined holocaust endgamers
who had overreached crude Middle Passage guards
all drunk on the milk of absolutism:
and now my dawn is come,
come at last to last eternity in recompense,
the cockcrow of a new birth, toughened
by your barbed tongue
that cuts through love's pledge like a keen razor
against the erect nipple

The Failed Courtship

At the road-spot where paths meet
and part, vows made and broken, I hailed
memories of our nuanced selves,
the conspiracy of history
in crass amorous venture, mouthing
crafted pledges on dust; of
the dream that failed before the cockcrow,
O Ngono of the wooded belt,
because you feminised my andro-soul, staging
your sneaky macho dreams on sinking sand:

the mystery that should have fruited every year
without the inconvenience of fear
over arch-point of the waterway,
soothing as a gentle wind's breezy spray;
a miracle for troubled humanity
behind steel blinds dicing unity,
remains famished as kindergarten milk,
when bits of my joy now fly in terracotta silk
and you are too old and stiff to understand
that only nightmares, like yours, grow on sand.

Naïve no More

Once, I was too naïve and
believed these holocaust clowns
weaving crudely tinkered swastikas
as patriotic yarn
around the nation's umbilical cord;

but now I know, as prosecuting witness,
how easy it is to die in this triangulated
contraption, crassly:

Auschwitz masquerades under equatorial sun
fail to scare even their cocoon
fancies, authorized in *point de presse*
orgasms—as if we did not live it
all before, in the '90s, remember?

Alabaster gods hate self-referent tags
to divinities that only bark, protecting
their bone with no flesh;
in the end, Kondengui shall offer
free tuition to the teeth-gnashing
rabble who re-course the River and talk trash
against the patriot seeking the ray.

February 11, 2017

Dem say today na big day for pickin dem,
But pickin wey go ever remain pickin,
Grow grey then *krobbo*,
Na ba'luck or na contri fashion?

I don see ghost dem dis days plenty
For sika say we no fit see ghost
And reason, according to Sasse grammar,
Na simply abuse of confidence!

No be logic, na only common-sense, again
For sika say all streets be dry,
Dry sotey pass dust for dry season,
Bad holiday for Market Massa and tax collector.

And youth don reach retirement age, you see na, with
Kind by kind kongossa about the future,
Even as leader of tomorrow, reason why
I vex plenty against Ngomna;

Year in, year out, the same okro soup
Without salt, not even fit for dog,
And they call'am unpatriotic if we say *ish*
And then rebel if, like now, I say *ngang*!

The Gospel of Peace

Peace is a blindfold for kindergarten
story-time today, the Fon's bedtime melody, even
as the community hallucinates in blinks of insomnia
and halleluiah manacles crack the brain open.

We have watched cine images, evening after dawn,
yawned over virused spaces of memory, hoping to forget,
because our world is falling apart, toyed by rascals,
and peace crusaders hammer the brass band astray.

That is why you don't ask again, comrades, why
anger showers our hopes like brimstones of woe, why
such ire is a luxury not to be possessed by the patriot
because gangsters hijacked the airwaves where peace is
        repackaged;

the *agent provocateur* garbed like katakata donman
to ensnare the patriot into dungeon of stone-breakers.

So the mind riots against itself, steeped
in pipedreams at imagined end of tunnel
and what else do we expect when the Fon is firewalled
and the password of peace, truth, crucified at noon?

Leaving the Promised Land

Promise disavowed, hunched
with sorrowed testimonies
like frills of flies on putrid glory
of these Alahmbit[1] whitewashers, across
the River. Steady my hand now,
you Watchers-on-Epasamoto,
that the horizon stays in focus, zoomed
anew in fig leaves, away
from the contingent years of tears
during which tales retold
and mistold on a tablet of dust
steeled my creative suffering, day by day.

---

[1] Literally, shitcountry

Shadows of Fear

Of late, from the shadows of raw fear,
dripping in crimson halleluiahs of a mortgaged vision,
        dystopian
heroes have wrenched the national imagination,
spiced a spin or two as habitual intro for primetime   news.

Scheming to plant dripping swastikas in every heart,
Morse whispers now seed dreams of tomorrow on new
        horizon.

Awkward enthusiasm
from those denied the joy of joy, how can we
harness the molten flow of things desired and denied?

Earth-filled skulls of Mbalmayo
or Matabelaland mock the Nkrumah hope
from the blotched page of history.
And finally, as if in a dream,
dynasts and their acolytes have bred dullards
who pale out in the vicinity of Lord Ludlum;
bloat every artery in the plastic progeny on dividends
from offshore trysts of the holy one percent
even as the plebe pave their path in rags and fronds.
It may take a day or a decade for the last kicks of the dying
        horse
to expire, still our hope and patience laminate
the lord's gastronomic vice.

In New York, they Only Talk, Always?

Guards of international diplomacy
scream to hoarseness, always: predictable,
some may say, as if more blood is requisite
for image of dream to emerge
from deferred byways.
Else, scribes of the Security Council
should have known that my Anglo-teardrop
is a crystal ball of worsted memories
on bank of the Mungo, auctioned for platitudes.

Today, a slave no longer speaks
of rivers because the memory of pain and the pain
of memory have been troughed into an endless renaissance
of new dawns with audacity.

Ah, my prophets are dead guys, indeed, feeding a lust
so simple that this carnation from this fresh tomb
teaches me once more that fear is man-made,
a distraction by the weak and cowardly
who voice Mille Collines pedagogy
in orgasmic madness of doomed
prophecies, hoarsing forth
a lame, Africanist vision
like a death whisper.

En Route to exile

The road to exile
is never a day's toil,
but the culmination of decreed burdens
that define the patriot,
fanged and fangled
by ideologues of a nameless creed...

How can I stay to this jingle
without rhythm,
ululations of denial, of deprivation,
that deny me and my kids
only grafting my name and voice
onto the chattered space

for this burden on my back,
child never to be unstrapped,
still seeking dawn and a name?

At the Crossroads

Now that days seem to have
wings, and my once fleety steps
only crawl on snail-slides:

where are the anchormen
and women in reserve
for assurance, when forwards and
backwards as in a bad dream

we keep postponing the signs of age,
you and I, still hoping for our day
in organic sequencing, shored
in hope of ever-new horizon

as the parrot-coo at dusk
augurs the fate of a people
caught in wilting veins entangled
at the fireside where story-time
echoes a monotonous pitch
without rhythm, stagnating?

Hail my Teacher, the Master

For those watery-mouth delinquents whose
official dribble, like their diapered woes,
mocked the sacred chalk
of nation-builders with sodomies of phallic talk:
see now, the rioting in the national den
after proud scribble of the pen!

Machiavelli communicants love their bombast
shows without lustre; which a day's collective fast
from Abakwa knolls to Victoria's white breakers
tames, remembering bedtime tales that were Weka's.

Leadership vacuum of innocuous gunocrats
now frills bottled angst showering like Nyamkweh gnats;
unnecessary *bras de feu*, if a genuine mentor
were to trough the molten bile of a terminator.

Even Christ confirmed the aftermath of cast dice,
submitting, contextually, to makers of lies:
the olive horizon we espy today, miraged
variation of what we, in good faith then, engaged;

renewed dream to be cut in Fako stone for all to see, how
we fared, hurt and cheated, before this blooming bough.

December 31, 2012

At crossroads of my life on needle-head
Having been struck by thunders I fed;

Always naive in embrace
Hoping to see God in every face;

A miraged promise in déjà-vu nightmare
Hiring standard-bearers in fanfare:

O, a ridiculous montage on national television
Where no patriot knows what to call vision!

New Year Resolution, 2013

I seek no fulfilment from common recognition
Of my raw voice.
Those with fine-tuned throats
Know best how to stir a vein
And pluck the world's fame, away from their hearts'
Need, but I seek no medal from conscripting hands.

The peace in me, unknown to watchers
Of signs for the hovering thousands,
And of wonders for the surging multitudes,
Spans eternity's endless rim, the shimmering frontier
Where God may yet linger, you know,
For my stubborn but yielding steps.

Ngoundou Day

The hired trumpeters again hail contrived misery
by which national poles are defined—
because God helps only those who pinch more,
even where they ploughed not, yet
free to tax and plunder,
dog must eat dog in the name of the Party and Fatherland;
else, why Bangemba breeds
chantillon dread diagnosed with nerves
beneath Nkoukouma's crumbless and gilded table
is puzzle for Senior Prophet Joshua,
that is, if we deny casualty status
by which we earn Bretton Woods accolades
while whorled emissaries,
hired still above ultra-market price
on taxpayer's sweat,
paint the paradisal gangway
and claim credit for uncreated artistry.

Communal Wisdom

My people know, untaught,
that mountains may stay aloof,
stay lonely and lonelied,
and even quarrel, skyward:
but they dancce
and embrace in the valley,
a rooted imperative as in Bangemba—
who then claims authority to conjure
tomorrow from what is merely seen, spoken and heard?

So I say, countri-pipou, let the parishioner
listen to unuttered mysteries
only felt in the vein, even as love,
when at God's divine gathering, Sheit[2]
denies the over-zealous believer
who demonised his Other and soul-mate, Satan;

even so as that handshake on rockface of Abakwa,
exposed party enthusiasts, fawning militancy,
their kind and viral consciousness,
after which constituted mafia families
groaned and retched, because Kwi'for[3]
and Morpuh reined in a twin decade of dread
because what was seen, spoken, and heard
defiled the heartbeat beneath
the caged contrivance.

---

[2] A compound pronoun, representing the composite Uncreated.
[3] Institution of authority in village politics; to be executed by the Morpuh, often with a crass comportment

Shit-Shiners *(for Gobata & TM)*

Those who deserve more than they are offered
spit on leprous visions that affirm mediocrity
in upper case, withdrawing.

That is why in this blighted claustrophobe,
white paint on muddy pavements always
announces the imminent entry of new gods
enthroned as shit-shiners,
but unable to tread upon our rags
for fear of mirror fates.

In the brief eternity of their reign, misery
shall groom their eulogies, rehearsed
in gilded epicurean trysts now, a skewered
affidavit, as they did swear,
not even good as compost dung
for Weka's sprouting vineyards.

A New Year Rose

for you, my Friend, whose
alabinda mystery
calms my disturbed artery
and I feel God's face
when I behold your veiling lace
now rolled back a bit
to show your Sheba spirit:
the end is also a beginning,
so I embrace it grinning.

Now that you are no longer there
(And all is gone that was fair)
Spirited away by a humble rascal,
(Who is fit to be christened a vandal)
Why should I withhold my songs,
(Whose echoes outlive golden gongs)
My wounded soul's tribute
(Even if the deaf think it mute)
Thankful celebration of you, my Friend,
(However our days and toils end)
Who sees beyond the Hubbub
(Where fungi grow on life's stub)...

Pre-Mortem for the Fatherland

This earth, my burden
and torture, living
in shackles and unwanted, where
the stranger is home-bred,
his brow broken at dawn
by the groans of dusk;

where the rebel is decreed,
a tag to veil a coffin-bearer's declamation
along the Commercial Avenue,
unveiling the rubbish under paint

because the new landlord, installed
without consensus,
is a tax-crazed, designer-made imp-skull, sweating after
Mother Weka's nugget;

and God watches, shackled too
by Hisherit's miscreation in Alahmbit,
fattened on clashing ideologies.

Ah-ya-mo Spot, Nkwen

The Sirens are still alive in Abakwa
on the descent of the old Finance House
where three roads meet
and clash, down the slope in neon trysts
for the wretched of the Nation,
forever touched by the Holy Spirit to have and give,
care of *two nkolo fap cent-ngoma*;

and Joseph Merrick's sanctuary
awaits the pala-pala ones on the cottaged knoll:
the incense from their pursed lips, and cherry-red,
coils into the anxious arrivant's eyes, twinkling off orbit
like rejected gifts of the Gods, trail
the paths of mystery unknown within the hungry soul,
forcing an awkward moment of rationalism
whether or not to surrender;

but the characteristic aroma-smile disarms
every a Super Makia heart that is weary
on the formal front where heroes are those who survive ring
       brutalities,
or affirm impeccable manners that seduce the social code
in cine atmospheres while adjusting the tie-knot in place
or the barber's latest trick in mirrored selves,
if only to feel the male they are not,
but still desire a dive into the lotus world.

And she coos in blinking smiles, come
ma Boy, come inside take communion, for God is
good all the time where two and three are
gather in His name. So no fear,

ma Baby, come, 'cos is good to be good, come na...

Marked and stoned verbally as the best way for us to
        vindicate self-guilt,
they only search for a different future
(if we but look and listen after the empty speeches)
beyond the civilised slough where communal wrong
is forgiven seventy-seven times seven times
(as new terminologies reinvent God in reality shows
enacting miracles with barracuda);
and remind us of what Christ might have said—
Other ye not, for we are all Other!

Nocturnal voices, booze-laced, and fumes infused,
conjuring distances and couched dreams at noon,
also hail God with Bacchic kaleidoscope: such tired voices—
and how can it be otherwise in a crazed culture
with lottery favours—whispering and cooing,
reminding you, and you recall the requiem sequence, that
tomorrow may never come; that life indeed is
now is life, a troubling overlap whose secret
is lodged in her cupped bosom and yours for just a booze and
        a promise
and a glimpse of the epiphanic horizon of knowledge,
if only you are man enough to espy the gates of paradise
where you stand, on a broken stair, finally, hesitant but eager,
because home is also where you find love and a soothing
        voice?

Un-Nodding Cock, 5a.m., after Nol Alembong

Those who archetyped the fruit
of Eden into universal injunction against
heart-throbs in jigi-jigi hemispheres,
(and even then had to oil it down ritual throats, discerning
jigi-jaga halleluiahs into endless dawns),
forgot Fuandem temporalities, their
fructifying mysteries at blur-moment,
today resurrecting as
cockcrow of parturition, and ordained
from glory of metaphors unknown
to makers of *the beginning*;

and in good ole Abakwa, always, the tolls at 5 o'clock
from the variegated knolls of divine mission
translate into rascals' own rhyme, surprised by dawn,
for popular nods, "Last time ... last time";

and because Nkum-Nkum Massa's
compass point—have you forgotten?—
indicates cultural footprints of desire,
of fear, and of the glory in nurturing
Eden where we stand; and Small Ngondere's *jigida*
reflects colours of the rainbow untagged
in the season of knowledge,
I confess recalcitrance
against the painted eternity and its *beginning*
whence God is a eunuch, *his* immanence and creed
an edited slate for kindergarten thrills,
admiring the apple, its beauty and relish,
but wondering about the teatsy manna.

Feeling Blank

Looking back from the habitual corner
at Carrefour de la Joie, the
prophecies and updated plans displaced,
the best we can do is admit the doom of a generation:
time surprised us, still
caught in the aroma of youth, our
feelers exploring endless beyonds
and their frilled frontiers
while this autocratic shadow shouts
new dawns, ever. Our days of idealism
are but cold ash in the hearth, when
we dared Nazi emissaries and their blunted tongue;
but today stare at defeat in upper case, and
toasting new King Kong embrace from
blokes with no brand future

until the blink, like collective therapy,
and shadows of dawn
sketch the horizon.

The Fall of a Colonel

Centuries of a skewered nightmare, mutating
as glorious stage-speech, and emboldened
by a golden pistol that forged an oasis community,
paradise from sand, but could not shoot a rat;
and humbled at last at mouth of sewage tunnel
where dreams of a Green or White Book
were doomed, long after Benghazi...

O, wordful child with stiff smile and no memory
of your chastened lore, your world without alien landmarks
except those you engraved, now mocks worshippers of
ludicrous ideology, because man pass you,
carry yi bag like combi, even for a deserved eternity.

O, sulky child, you dreamed a nightmare in candy packs;
else how could you celebrate with blood-sucking miscreants
whom death rejected, forever hiding
behind the Ayon Curtain, and drugging struggling humanity
with bits of misquotes from angrier but sensible Marx?

If only you knew that those who forge ideology
also toast aeons of milk and horny
in cactus arena of global merry-milking;

like the gathered misery around your *kata-kata* brow
which stirs my phlegm, dirged child, now
eulogised by new disciples of stagnant Pan-
Africanna, along paths long gone fallow;

your peers refusing to read signs of your demise,
and rehearsing your marshal rhetoric

in favoured *temps mort* of their prolonged misery
while I watch, here in Abakwa, where the sun always rises.

For Mandela

We mourned the Madiba's lauded demise
at midnight of absent watchers of the land
the way we celebrated his release
from tubercular fangs of Victor Vorster,
with snarls of hypocrisy, the
weird masks for cine witnesses.

Those whitened teeth that charmed
masters of doublespeak, conjured peace
and security for Nubialand in the warlord's
inner chambers, asphyxiating
Afrique their Africa from Paris and her walls of mirrors—
how they reflect new captives on old turf now,
repeating the old cheap game of
nord-mali-zation,[4]
dubious broker of peace,
sower of discord.

And away from the plastic smiles
and the predictable parchment against Bangui's latest slave,
Pelican wings in flight belie
history's contingent sentence, *vers* Charles de Gaulle.

Final stride of Madiba in peaceful gasp,
man more than man, as we look
on, stunted by shackles of falsehood,
stupid iniquities of what is easily said in

---

[4] This coinage, Nordmalization, rendered in French, was coined (at least as far as I know) by a comedian on the private television channel, Canal 2 in Cameroon, when he was ridiculing French policy in the North of Mali.

swollen adjectives, mimicking doom.

Valiant fighter who defied jail, he liberated
jailer too, and screened new horizons
in rainbow embrace, redefining theorised zones.
Recalcitrance enthroned at last,
some said, already patching the wounds
of decadal miseries into hymns for Black Yesus
whose managed anger, frilled in rainbows of
the new birth, voiced a prophesy.

My Chairman

My own Chairman
rascally enthroned in Fuandem
mysteries undiluted, along wriggling knolls
and their spiralling glory:
the pepper-soup table of nib-visionaries
is redeemers' constituency
seeding hope to a beaten people;

din of the maddening crowd
is God's other spice
to diagnose lunacy, a national
condition to doom Marion's fields of plenty.

This thrill of mediocre lead-singers, chorusing
doom in speeches, again signals
eternal damnation at end of the tunnel:
even if your handshake is gloved, still
a hybridizing ploy in Gaullist oils,
after which Weka's progeny, garbed
in blackest black in memoriam,
will be endless dirge-singers
in a ruffians' den?

My Salute for You, Abouem à Tchoyi

Apoungtsoung'he[5] na my name, Sah,
Because like my papa and mama before me,
I no be get person for give me bread and tea.

I no be know say as Govnor for Gbeuya and Abakwa
You be also be schoolboy with pencil and notebook
For find out why shit for Foumban di still smell today!

My people get worry too much Shey, because
False political prophets dem don turn contri upside-down,
With Mbelle-khaki dem for all corner, say make we shur'up,
      else...

Even today sep-sep, Mola, for this new Contri Sunday
Wey even fly and mosquito get to stay for their own *ntang*
Radio and TV di still preach lie-lie motif, like say we be fools.

So you bi good man, Iyeuh, my own very man, and Papa
God know say na true, when I hear facts from you like true-
      true
Man of God, only say you di talk for *moumou* them!

After Maguida spoil my heart, when yi talk like blind God,
You turn the same heart into yori-yori sunrise,
So I thank you, and say God bless!

Even bookman, the Prof of Profs—habba, water pass garri!
He too turn kata-kata fellow and talk with water for mop
Like say big book and power fit pass common-sense.

---

[5] Literally a child with no carer; an orphan.

And yi combi, Massa for Wigs, sworn to truth,
But, abi, okro make yeye with yi tongue?
Or na just bad heart in the name of the fatherland?

I be dey Swine Quarter yesaday for take one for the road
And one filosofa tell me: "Don't worry my pickin; is good to
            be good
Because no bad condition made by man is permanent…"

Now I dey Sisia Quarter di wait make dis big Contri Sunday
            pass
Before I go back for Swine Quarter for hear how we di
            survive the peace;
And with no matango for pray on-top now, I salute you,
My Govnor, after my filosofa:

"Papa God sabi why yi make the darkest hour for come
            before dawn
So no fear, I tell you, get hope say sun go so-so rise
            tomorrow
Even if Yaounde and yi disciples dem paint the sky black".

For a National Uncle

Like farts of a dazed god, your lips rattle presidential
bikutsi on Bull Frog milk, blot of Njenka dreams,
hired to twist the course of the River with a cloned
      membrane;
you choke the plebe with broken consonants
in translation: rain-
soaked, dead stumps for incumbent
halleluiah, your orgasmic
dread, croaking the miseries
of your wilting soul, cashiered.

Ah, the Fourth Estate, auctioned to ageist
props of your *chaud gar* flair, rehearsing
Squealer doublespeak with Bitzer
brains, and a Googled letterhead which
announces presence with no roots.

Michael West gave us meaning
that was meaningful when we were still searching
for the sun across concentric landmarks;
but your fomol-freshened breath
withers the shoots of hope
(from our dailies and telecasters)
planted on martyred spots of the umbilical
root. Oh, impertinent child from Sawa dreams
miscarriaged at point of communal expectations, your
hybrid voice trails contours of doom, trembles
as pure aesthetics of Bangmeba shit-cleaners, browbeats
peer prognostics from your ivory tower
for promise of stale *bobolo* and *mbongo-chobi*, when
all that is left is the past tense of shit.

Once I hailed you, like now I seek to nail you
as we await the cockcrow before confession, when
you shall blink in blank horizons of denial, haunted by
hawks of deontology and hugging
the misery of your crafted voice
with no audience;

and we shall remember that you
cut Angwafor's voice, and then Mola Litumbe's,
at ritual of coin-flipping in Gbeuya,
so your progeny shall know a traitor's shame.

For Achebe, A Tribute

When things fall apart, the
centre finally holds,

a post-
independence logic, branded
in Nubialand

where the face of misery
defines more charity from across the Suez:
in the strangled noises, and
thinking of the beginning and
refusing to think of the end; and

bowing to octogenarians of the gimmickry,
whose only good is a stagnating membrane
and a visionary scam,

paying homage to a Grand Master travesty
that spells God upsidedown
or in reverse, preferably,

we begin
to understand how
anthills survive
in the savannah of our post-independence galore—
or do they?

For Ali Mazrui, a farewell

Neo-PanAfricanist who
conceptually decolonised
the positioned mythologies (their gory oracles of pelf
        contorting
even as they visaed his stipend), after Anta Diop;
illuminated anew by Wiredu
and Gobata candles,
a new insight!

Aristotle was only one pathfinder,
not an end, and the rains still beat us today
because we have waxed our ears with bars from itune
headsets, glossed our eyes with fine-country
looking glasses; and our skin no longer shines
with *minyanga* lotion that conjures *yori-yori* paradise,
flavoured in bridal dawns that never doubt
the community's rendezvous with tomorrow.

Speechy messiahs have embalmed our fate,
so we need not worry about the future;
and harried through Bretton Woods conditionalities
for catch-up séances
of dodokido games in nation-building,
we hail our doom in Four-G sophistication.

And a continent sags (have you even noticed
the death-jerk monitored and controlled from donors'
sweet talk and prognostics?), confronting renewed miseries
with every dawn; rejecting shrine-ritual
because Jesus is the only way, *they* claim,
even after Okigbo had helped us trough

other complementary estuaries in cultural selfhood,
after Biafra: bright brains still try to convince us
that a universal ancestor acquits relative cultural iniquities,
another catch-up theology which peeps into the Hubbub
after Galileo and Hawkin and claims kudos unmerited;
that idol worship is a fact only out of Church consciousness,
a convenient rat-trap that cannot catch the wooden things on
        church walls,
even after Bakingili's infernal vomit (we are reluctant to face
        the truth
for fear it sets us free!) exhausted its ire
on the kerb and a footstep from the sea God's abode.

For Abouem à Tchoyi, Afterthought

Oracles are heeded to
in arrears, after floods of blood
have conquered our reinforced barracks of hate
and blackmail. I salute
your courage in this lotus den
where siblings scheme to disappear
each other, for favour.
Oracular tongue, guiding
the roofless heads against cactus
storms, I hail you!

Ah, the burden of memory reviving, when
that day, decades ago, when Nico
Mbarga was the continent's lone celeb,
as we crowded the precincts of Community Hall,
the crass crash against your official screen
summoned regular phlegm: the young
and the old were booted by khaki
ruffians, reinforced from across the Matajem,
until Town Hall summons again
humbled authoritative arrogance,
and you emerged from the place
a true man of the people.

And today bards sing your name
in brazen colours across a land where it is easier
for camel hooves to sail through a needle's eye
than to hear a word of truth from incumbent lips.

Soyinka's Tears Today

Yes, in the beginning was the Word, but uttered across
cultural horizons, in various tongues,
none masterful.

But exported and imported words
from men of God,
and women of God;
from men Letters,
and women of Letters
poorly copied and wrongly encoded
(only chaff and slime in modelling grain and mud of God
whose smithy embraces the muddy and digitised spheres),
claimed and still claim vision with looking glass, whip, and
        goggles.

Indeed, irate Ogun mass-servants have decried
the essence of rot inherited and propagated
with its champion strawmen;
have been cursed by regime snipers for the inconvenient
        truth
on a blessed but graft-doomed patch.

And in the aftermath of storytellers we love,
the grammar was bound to be embarrassing
to those who failed to see the tainted beginnings
when Ogun fires toughened the vocalic tendons that became
the terror of dirtied ways, the shorer of enabling dreams
against ever new Aso-rockers in Rockefeller Disney bubble.

Was a creek-trip of that autobio-interpreter who denied the
atavistic mystery not warning enough of what was to come?

No wonder Brother Jero sneezed at the holy merchants,
their concordant stupidities that auction God, while
Kadiye rainmakers and their cheer-gatherers in amphitheatres
reinvent doom, and curse Madiba rays of exposure, as the
        restive nip
always seeks the ritual gourd and camwood for indelible drip
to forge the future we lost.

Abiku Revisited

Child of eternal returns, river of endless meanings,
as long as the umbilical cord lasts; as long
and varied as the tongues that speculate your mystery
like *moni mboom-pa*, my own babble, but only
a tip of the post-Babel anthill;
and reminds us of how we once were, probably,
a mixture of hues and fragrances
that form the *jigida* flare, arc of the rainbow. But the elements
and human fear and greed pulled us apart,
and still do, into conjectured paths

and you remain a child of mystery,
coy and bold and elusive ever,
despised and dreaded, but never decimated.

Possessor of death—and of life too?—beyond
scientific minds that squeeze hypotheses
into sickler fullstops, when myth and memory
know better, only a bit cloudy, for now.

How can we fathom the reaches
of your feelers, ever shimmery, after
new horizons and their dawns?
Ogbanje discourse for instance, as shortcut
to pacify doubt? Or, still, Ngingerou othering
as in Mulatto, Albino, Moukala, or Bon-Blanc;
and of Baby Suggs' granddaughter, angry returnee,
child of the River, 'cos thin love ain't? Proud
ignorance is our only fear, and pride our doom.

Child of many worlds and varied names,
none benign in the least, only demonised
by ignorance and fear of knowledge,
the most of our heroics, I salute you:
we have invented meanings to deny you and ourselves;
accepted other meanings that camouflage you and our faces
until the mystery of life and death and rebirth
mocks us, always accepting and believing,
unable to remember, see, and accept.

But still, you point the way...

Reminiscences of the Sabbath

Conned by the guardians of hell's smithy
to keep it holy, for fear
of what should not be feared, forgetting
that you see and define God
only where you stand;

we called forth the days and the nights after
Gregory's intellectual scam, a hebdo
convenience that aligns the stars
in sophisticated magic against
lunar relativity where we stand to see God.

Today, in the craze of virtual presences, their divine
mystery chipped into our blood, and anchored
to the global system on the superhighway
where difference is only a fraction of nought,

the urgency for a new launch pad burdens the soul
that hungers for a dawn whose rainbow ray
summons us into the shrine, to pray.

On Day of the Sun, as commanded, after Norse
vicissitudes in Roman gear infected igneous limbs of
        Stonehenge
and rushed across the Sahara in hybrid procreation,
dousing our brains as we nod and nod in denial
that Creation has many calendars,

you robe your sins to church, hymn
away the hypocrisy that strangles every new shoot,
and thereafter flutter home, a spiritual sim and

halleluiah miracle made evident in renewal, another
hebdomadal fantasy of crass spirituality,
Rome's modelled Jerusalem breeding confusion.

But keep Contri Sunday holy, one out of three we remember,
or three into one under these new suns, says a new voice,
when we knew God where we stood, awaiting
the trumpet sounds from top of the Fako, with
regrets for errors of the past, and each a bough
for the fallen in unmarked spots.

After reading W.B. Yeats, Again

My cultural ancestors are draped in rainbow frills
of botched dreams in phoenix hue, their mirage frontiers
shimmering from horizons of my hybrid heart, where
a terrible beauty always counts the hours
toward the midnight hope-in-Mukong.

Yes, who can be neutral here, after these strident voices
of hate-incarnate, vowing to make *soya* of our innards
served with chopsticks from Beijing? Verbal sandbags, as
shields, to shore the iniquities of a few demented fellows
who grip the lectern with arthritis fingers and conscript our
        attention
with august promise of dust and more blood?

I lulled in pacifist hope unexhausted, proud to be a patriot,
conscripted too to the Luther King creed
to change only with olive branch fervour, but now know
in my wounded heart that the Patriot, kin
to the Exile and the Rebel, is groomed on promises
either in the cradle or at crossroads:

I hail phoenix stirrings for my Rebel
within Kondengui womb of concrete rust, dreaming rainbows
for my progeny, served *mingwin* for breakfast,
kurukuru at noon, and Pinyin biscuits along the way
across the dried hills, toward the green valley;
or across the frontier, seeking seat
at New York's Round Table where despots still ensure
stillbirths in Bangemba, gloss over mass graves, or conjure
        Nambia space
for a Sunrise Baby-Girl in cyborg hemispheres

with no apology for every holocaust spot.

Feeling this lust so simple, yet so enduring,
I hail my name where I stand,
nurtured by my inheritance, confident
that this night of pain unmerited shall last
only a blink of man's eternity
in cacophonous dreams and broken promises
from those who stare, unblinking, at shadow
of a dream they slaughtered, and with hope
that a dawn will come with a name that is mine.

The Making of Genocide

'L'Etat a le droit de violence légitime' Hermann Messinga, Journalist, on Afrique Media—19.06.2018

For those still in doubt, because the newscaster
on TV wears a plastic smile to vaporise our fears
at the crossroads of a crumb-less day:

that is when the United Nations
barks over the convivial discourses
of a neoliberal leech

(whose emissaries
bear polonium 2010 in the digitised portmanteau
and distributes crackers to kids in
kindergarten *à la* Bolore)

and at dusk dispatches
casual observers in a blend of misery,
touting preventive decromancy in the injury time
of hope-betrayed, when those with dreams
cling only to a straw memory
and remember a God who no longer smiles
on a tattered humanity, dispersed
across the frontier.

Bloc-conspiracies, perfected since heydays
of the Old Pilot, who spun verbs of enchantment
across the diplomatic chessboard
in renewal of their tribal heritage and galore
shortly before Versailles negotiated this
miserable future in the absence of the victims

(crassly positioned in a broken scale, birthing
the scarecrow dawns which adjectives no longer
approximate),

spell doom in crimson marks
when Resolution One-Million-Zeros will hatch
another Darfur to the glee of the toasting coterie.

The Sanaga, Midnight

I crossed the Sanaga again, the jerky
dread of bridges returns, bridges whose walls
are spiked with verbal cactus, forged
from snarls of brotherhood in a lost dawn.

I felt the surge of nausea, giddied
by the dark dread, sluggishly gnawing at my soul:
primal remembrances for knowledge
in the garden of knowledge, and the sulphur embraces!

Jesters had looted my hope, auctioned
the future to French and then Beijing weevils,
after autochthonous fraternities had cheerled
the beginning of ruin in a fancy of pops and froths;

nation-building straw castles on sand, roofing
the nightmare before planting the stick-pillars,
but now I hear chants of new masons
with bulging muscles, return of exiled kindred

and who shall dare their infra stare
after the banks of memory are shored,
and the lore of Bangemba restored
to universal acclaim and fanfare?

Prayer

Yesterday's pains firmed me,
Now your nightmare
At cross-point of the future:

Tomorrow is
Forever and eternity is
Now that I oil my throat
In *mbaghelem* rhythm
And Fako blasts of victory
With no firemen to save the bridge—

Hear my voice, O Herod,
And lessen the pain of your intransigence.

Ghost Towns

Dr King would have certified this plebeian conspiracy
against the owners of power with no authority,
after gangsters, chauffeur-driven in tainted convoy,
talk to whitewashed walls and rows of plastic from
China, because no town-hall miracle
manifests from the rostrum where high-table brains
douse guttered ire, leaping for new horizon,
a genuine plebiscite.

In this Darwinian gyre where the vacant streets
offer only remnants of rhapsody the day before—the straw-
         shacks
of buy'am-sell'ams, the iron-barred shops of myriad confetti,
the lotus spots in neon and pops where youth was reinvented,
a future imagined in frilled dreams—but now witness the
alert sentries positioned at street corners to fire out of sight[6]
and forestall another Biafra headache, and sirens forge a
         symphony,
the new lullaby for the aged kid in pre-nursery;

a stray dog crawls along the sidewalk, tail between hind-legs,
sneaks around the butcher's, sniffs after yesterday's memory
and sulks away on trembling legs, a habitual fate, with
not even a vulture in sight to await its feast of bones;

and this midnight silence of tombs at noon cajoles
only requiem-mongers on national television, pipers
of the national brass band, whitewashing

---

[6] 'Fire out of sight': Wole Soyinka's ridiculing of the military at the start
of the Biafra crisis in Nigeria; see *The Man Died*.

autocratic rubbish in verbal nuances, hoping
we shall not dare to remember.

The Exodus

As if we did not hear of the horrible tales beyond the frontier,
how long- or short-sleeve designers
served the warlord's Faustian paradise,

a frenzy of carted migrants
toward the hydra's embrace, as internally
displaced, and new grammar grows on misery;

the travel agencies choked with material anxieties
and the centre appears to hold
in the lapse of new configurations
sprouting on blood.

The Curfew

Hour of the curfew tolls again
atop the spired-monuments, from Big Mankon to
St. John, echoing the harried labours;
reverting pupils of weary hawker or clerk
notice only the haze
and clang of misery, patterned as peace and order,
for the evening news;

no more the gentle farewell, as evening
freezes suddenly, and we begin to learn
how to roost even before the hen
on her branch, making peace and order
a hollow laugh.

The Poet *(for Colbert, Q&A)*

In moments of tongue-darkened stars,
he strings words of ancestral lore against
suckers of the land; cotton-stuffed skulls
who hijack communal vision (as beggars of the peace
they slaughter), sneaky rapists at noon…

No prophet, yet prophecy is his play thing, scanning
amoebic souls for shreds of meaning, where pelf
opens the gates of paradise; chronic harbinger
of hope even for lips that swell with foul thoughts;
their Dracula fangs biting truth, squeezing
the juice of the commonweal
into midnight conduits, where
Munzu still stands, my messenger.

Once from an Aghem manger
I hailed a rainbow eternity, heard Songo
Trobo vibrate rain and sun intercourse
in the full moon of Nkoh dispensations against dirty hearts…

Ah, mystery of dry lizard on lean stalk
and sacred word from healthy hearts…

So how can I lose faith, deny tomorrow
and its fear-thawing rays, when we gather
around the communal court yard, to see through
the darkened clouds, summon
those who speak out too inconveniently
to keep guard, because
only bereaved lips know where
redemption songs flow?

Still I Dream

When the darkest hour seems to be around
forever, and Trump and Gutiérrez are silenced
by the programmed considerations, veto or no veto,
of the fattened aftermaths-in-reconstruction,

I still dream—

and see the fleeting face
of nature's glory
bequeath a smile for aeons unknowable—of

the flickering light, its ray a promise,
beyond the gloom...

The Final Moment

The masquerades are awake, frenzied
in blind purpose against despoilers
whose charms conjure murky horizons;
the Gods would stand by those with clean hearts
to cleanse the shit of the decades.

We have burdened kids to mature
prematurely, and who
in the moment of rising masquerades
shall save them, who, from the horrors
of uncushioned experience!

Sunrise of tears, and the reprieve: no more
the eunuchs of a chorused mentality
even though we walk through flame and murk,
the dawn in rainbow, ours to hail,
the name, proudly lettered, ours to call!

Aghem Boy, After Q&A, December 15, 2018
(for Jay-Eff)

A lie is a terrible thing to
groom, for scanty feast of unbecoming;
you weary me even with your legitimate voice,
meant to balance the debate, chart the way.

Dearth of self-knowledge,
or mere back-scratching in Eppesse-*ntswa'a* sessions,
hailing the hangman in ton-ton macoute conclaves,
an ideological mimic on edge of the cliff?

Suck your dry bones, brother, syringed
with fomol; watch the starless skies of Nkoh keening,
the streaks of dread against the evil-bringers
and continue to dine with wooden gods
after the German Farm
and WADA
and the Weh airstrip
and the Menchum, for
yours is the glory now…

Those seven mosquitoes, *sans domicile
fixe*, and emissaries of tomorrow
whom you spited, as they voiced twilight
from Ndefcam soundscapes, know that
only blistered soles and palms peg the future
you sweat to erase with hollow adjectives.

And these pillars of sand you wedge, planted
from the watery lips in ballot seasons, and mortared
in smokescreens of barbed wire

around the communal brain,
how can you lie to yourself
and still hope to snore at night?

In Memoriam *(for Prof P.K. Mbufong)*

All our adjectives accrue to nought
Now, when the breathe is gone, bought
And sold in this pregnant season,
When arrogance bereaves reason!

It may not be for the dead that we cry,
Potential targets too, of the crass lie
That peace or piss can be decreed
In fattened verbs of a strong breed.

And molten anger dissolves into fearful dawn
While collegiate silence walks the tearful lawn
Along which he too read the shimmering future,
Now robed in darkened shades of a glossed culture.

And yet, these incredible bars of the Master
Restore me, Amadeus miracle after dark day's disaster;
The Requiem's eternal rest for you, Boss, when tears mete
And aggrieved souls their tears and laughs complete.

Epilogue: Menka Blues

(To those who know why they cry)

> 'All changed, change utterly,
> A terrible beauty is born'.
> —W.B. Yeats

I

Storymakers never hear their names
archived at the moonlit séance
of community stock-taking, where
the frenzied masquerade returns, drunk
with the passion that silenced creative agitation; shatters
the scheduled press conference where
falsehood is auctioned in subdued bargain; offers
the language of the deaf mute
to the makers of death who hover around the mic
dripping gallons of piss and feed on their Faustian porridge,
twirling the adulterine moment as eternity's eggshell
on the hammered lectern.

Contrived dawn at The Star, as the morning hope
vanished with lightening dread of conspirators,
counting their rusted pieces of silver,
having eavesdropped into plebeian secrets.

My doubts have finally caught up with me, in
this commissioned dawn of amazing gracelessness, when
genocide is dressed in national colours, seeding
the wind with questions unanswered.

Iniquities of the chosen and of the blessed
may raise no eyebrows because

those who suck midnight blood of sacrifice
still trade invincibility on mirage sceptre.

II

Weaned of the milky talk that bred dullards at pole position,
my doubts haunt me still, with comic mockery, patriot
and pacifist that was, now witness to the rapacious gang
that feeds on the foetal chunks of sacrifice,
seasoned caviar shipped VIP across the Matajem, duty-
      free,
and served with Mouton Cadet at Jesus Restaurant:
See how they stoop to walk with terminal francaemia,
after the latest transfusion and bypass;
hear how they croak to affirm a lie
at another *point de presse* harried in contingent glory;
and gesture like a man of the moment in gilded gandoura
à la Kontchou—brain banks of the system and
gangsters of a doomed ideology; snorting over
their parboiled broth, breeding chaos
on chaos for only a tickling sensation around the groin.

Mass-servants of the ridiculous show, who
steal from their own pockets to make a name, we
know them, the deified Akamentsos with blood of kins
on their hands, like the hired Ntumfors,
sporting broken chicken feathers on *shiinkar*, and hoping
to make the dead walk across the Matajem,
if only to flatter the godfather—vision-giver
and taker—in ritual of blood and more blood,
to dispense a pantheon stool
in Alahmbit with bloody skyline.

III

A change gonna come, yes,
to coincide with the next birth-cry, the
umbilical relay in our survival; after
the severed bridge, the forgotten memory,
trough to a new dawn, to claim my name.

I, alone, know the troubles I have lived, every
nerve pulled to the limit as prosecution witness;
my tears, my cries in this echoing dusk, no more
as mere existentialist jargon between cover pages, but
the fructifying secret to my survival
against the humpback coterie conning
death in a glee of vagrancy: our folks in cream toupees,
and in league with chalk-holders, crafted the petition,
the wake-up gong that echoed in the varsity wails in Gbeuya.

Tinto vindicated Ako-Aya, even as 'Ayah vs. Them' affirmed
Weka tutelage against a toady brain refusing to grow;
Menji, like a manger in a valley of green, weaved Fuandem
incense across the stubborn hills
until Belo resurrected Afo-Akom's groin rascal at crossroads
with wrathful finger and sword against the guilty (who
breed death from Eviland), relayed
via Ngonnso's shrine on the primitive side of Nkum, where
Kibarankoh's sperms stalk the death-bringers:
they are not Wisemen today who come from the East, no,
with infested handshake, conjugating prophecies of death
before the promise land at this darkest hour,
as Tisagli monitors the horizon, cautious, and in anticipation
of Ateng'he's diagnosis from the pool where tadpoles breed.

IV

We have burdened our children in kindergarten
with knowledge too much too soon, shown
them the sights that blind a Gorgon, rehearse
Auschwitz tactics with acid and flame, brandished
as candy in their dream gardens, and
still call it a fatherland in 'Citizenship'
or 'Civics and Ethics' in our mimic pedagogy
where the toy canister scars tomorrow's membrane,

as they grow old at a blink of
generous floodlight in the hastened ritual of innocence
on a borrowed name, sucking French candies.

In the effervescence of the Republic, cut and pasted,
our definitions have expired amidst the grief, a grammar
of sinister homogeneity, and Larousse
suddenly a hoarse voice amidst the panic, and
the time of innocence a nightmare.
No more the birthdays, ticking the calendar; no more
the knock-doors at start of dusk, conjuring generations;
and no more the nuptial halleluiahs already
peeping into eternity at postcode GZ, because
words have lost their juice and mortar
in toothless mouths that spell God in reverse;
only dust unto dust in the transgression of meaning,
a national refrain for the dispossessed in Bangemba,[7]
the Patriot seeking a frontier and a home and a name.

---

[7] A compound of 'Bangem' and 'Ngemba'. See my play, *Searching for Bate Besong* (Langaa, 2014).

V

I have lost my equanimity, the pods
of faith and of innocence, raped by arid nouns
from plastic lips, their drudgery a menace
in the crimson aftermath of eerie corn-popping.

A sulphurous dawn greets my greetings, offering shrivelled
shoots from my earthy voice.

These smiles from lipless masks that seemed soundful
            yesterday,
hearken to their justification of crass policy;
these handshakes from claws made nerveless
by countless bypass tinkering around the breast cavity,
feel their cold numbness of death, the passive smile
glued to the cold-fats faces, tolled
from spire of St. John's;

and the answer still blows in the wind
after the formalin giggles at diplomatic teatime, when
Americans begin to flee (if you remember the sign and drill)
and the hawk circles the target perimeter.

Where are the kinsmen with shifty eyes—backsliders
and turn-coaters, crossing the dirt-couched carpet—
who showed the preying stranger in tattered moccasin
the way to the homestead and the shrine,
for thirty pieces of counterfeit?

VI

As I weep and garner strength in weeping,
Oh, Chukiyuh,[8] impertinent child caught
at crossroads of your stronghead in The Star, see
now, Nfor Bamenda's tears from the hereafter,
and even Man di Loss finally admits
that man fit loss money, but also people,
to a demented force cutting corners, enmasked,
changing the course of the Mungo tributary.

Beyond tribulations of the darkest hour,
I scratch away the cobwebs from my hurting eyes,
survey the desecrated space of Bangemba
(which no press conference will camouflage,
the filthy truth of shit-shiners, after Gobata, hoping
to postpone tomorrow's ray by a few seconds);

witness to the birth of a prophecy, where I stand,
on blotched spot of The Star massacre, calling
out the names we know.

In anticipation of this season of resurrection, we
declare our credentials at confirmation ceremony:
we are who we are, builders from scratch, after
the earth-cleansing rituals, fuelled live on Radio
Sept Collines, whose vision for-never hollers a broken
Pan-Africanism with lips swollen by greed and hate.

And in the lapse of silence made meaningful,
Nwuoueplai lives to tell the tales about yesterday
and young Chikibana, the inheritor of dance floor shoes,

---

[8] A person, usually a child, who fails to heed advice until it is too late
(Mungaka)

feels Bottle Dance rhythms on the bereaved tongues, when
Ground Zero breaks the cuffs around the brains,
sows hope on a string of wailing voices,
the parched throats awaiting the cockcrow
and the nectarine dawns, after
the Iscariots who sprout on a fattened tale
must have been tamed, my tear's amen.

The End

is the endless tale for survival ever since
we learned to blink with one eye, against the Sphinx:
we should *emerge from* the forest
finally, to seek a new beginning;[9]
the end is also a fresh beginning
and promise now, of eternal rest.

---

[9] The first two verses here are modified from the last dialogue in *Apocalypto*, a film which, considering the first excerpt at the start of this collection, represents the modern epic of human journeying for identity.

Printed in the United States
By Bookmasters